THE MINI BOOK OF
GOLF

BY CHRIS STONE

T0364054

Running Press
Hachette Book Group
1290 Avenue of the Americas, New York, NY 10104
www.runningpress.com
@Running_Press

First Edition: April 2010

Published by Running Press, an imprint of Perseus Books, LLC, a subsidiary of Hachette Book Group, Inc.

The Hachette Speakers Bureau provides a wide range of authors for speaking events. To find out more, go to www.hachettespeakersbureau.com or call (866) 376-6591.

The publisher is not responsible for websites (or their content) that are not owned by the publisher.

ISBN: 978-0-7624-3815-0

CONTENTS

INTRODUCTION

▼

Do you love golf but are sick of the weekend drudgery? The draining five-hour rounds, the inclement weather, the prohibitively expensive green fees, the costly equipment, the archaic dress code, and, above all, the hopeless inconsistency of your swing all add up to a miserable experience. You took up the sport for exercise but nowadays you are often forced to ride on a golf cart to get around the course.

Well, despair no longer; thanks to *Desktop Golf*, your passion for the game is sure to be revived. The beauty of mini golf is that it can be played anywhere. The dress code for mini golf is more relaxed—and there are no expensive green fees. Plus, you won't have to endure eighteen holes wrestling with the unpredictability of your swing.

Desktop Golf comes with two clubs, a felt fairway with one hole and three marked distances—to give you three, four, and five "par holes"—two golf balls, and sand for your "bunkers." It's light and easy to use, and a lot more compact than your full-size equipment. In fact, mini golf could turn into the greatest stick-and-ball craze of the twenty-first century, but don't just take my word for it. Get playing!

A BRIEF HISTORY

Golf has always been a difficult game to master, but that has never dented its appeal. The sport taps into a strangely compulsive human desire—the urge to swing a stick in order to strike an object at rest on the ground.

Where it all started, nobody really knows, but it certainly began, at least in a primitive form, a long time ago. There is a record of a golf-like game having been played in Loenen aan de Vecht, in Holland, on February 26, 1297. The Dutch players used a stick and a small leather ball; players hit the ball towards a target several hundred yards away. By the fifteenth century, golf in a more recognizable form was being played all along the east coast of Scotland (some say bored shepherds invented golf by hitting smooth pebbles into rabbit holes with their crooks for fun). However, in 1457 James II of Scotland tried to ban it, the suggestion being that it

stopped youngsters doing more con-
structive things with their time—
archery practice, for instance.

A century later, Mary, Queen of
Scots—the first known female golfer—
introduced the game in France (her
helpers, young military cadets, gave
rise to the term "caddies"). In fact,
among the charges brought against her
while incarcerated in England under
Elizabeth I was that of playing golf the
day after her husband had been mur-
dered. But even the hapless Mary's exe-

cution failed to deter the early golfing pioneers. Much like today's golfers, once bitten by the golf bug, they were forever smitten.

By the mid-eighteenth century, the earliest golf clubs in England and Scotland were being established. A further significant development was the introduction, in 1754, of the first official "Rules of Golf;" there were only thirteen rules, but they represented a step towards the meaningful codification of what was then still a fairly chaotic game. Ten years later, the Society of St. Andrew's Golfers determined that a round of golf should consist of eighteen holes.

Golf courses soon started to spring up around the British Empire from India to Australia, with the game finally taking off in the United States in the second half of the nineteenth century.

The rest, as they say, is history. But times have changed—and, with them, the fashions, the demographic of players, the sophistication of equipment and, perhaps more than anything, the financial rewards for professional golfers. At the first US Open in 1895 the total prize fund was $325; in 2008 it was $7.5 million, with a cool $1.35 million being awarded to the winner, Tiger Woods.

Of course, a weekend hacker like you will never get a sniff of that action, so why not consign your clubs to the attic and instead devote your spare time to mini golf? No professional golfer has ever managed the Grand Slam of winning all championships in a year in majors and yet, with a bit of practice, you could achieve just that—without leaving the house.

PLAYING MINI GOLF

▼

Like standard golf, the miniature version can be played in either matchplay or strokeplay formats. Games can be held over three, six, nine, eighteen, thirty-six, or seventy-two holes, depending on the time you have available and the level of competition. If you have a spare five minutes, you can easily fit in three holes; seventy-two is the accepted format of serious strokeplay competition, and it requires stamina and concentration.

Basically, you can set up and play on any flat surface. With mini golf, there's no need to phone the club three weeks in advance to book a tee time. *Desktop Golf* is totally portable, so whether you're at home, at the office, in a department store, or on the train— if you fancy a quick "nine holes," roll out the course and away you go.

At the office, players are encouraged to book a meeting room during the lunch hour, close the blinds, and hold championships. If it's a quick game you can play under your desk. Or, if you're feeling adventurous, take the elevator and play holes on different levels.

There are ample opportunities for matches at home, too. Why not make full use of your house and yard to set a stiff challenge? The front nine could include a tough par five up a staircase, a picturesque par three over water (a full sink) in your bathroom, and a dogleg par four that bends around the side of the sofa. Then you could head into the back yard for the second nine, battling against the varied challenges of long grass and concrete paving. Of course, all this will take place to the probable bemusement of your family and neighbors—but don't let that deter you.

Rules of the Game

- Golf is a game of tradition and impeccable etiquette, and while mini golf might not have the sophistication of its mother sport, certain standards should be maintained. Smart attire and cleated shoes are encouraged. No jeans or sneakers, please.

- ◆ Shouting out or otherwise maliciously distracting your opponent is prohibited, although if you're cunning there are ways around this (see below).

- ◆ If your ball goes in a hazard (for example, a coffee mug on your desk, the sink in your bathroom) your penalty will be one stroke, at a distance of two club lengths not nearer the hole. If ball goes out of play (falls off your desk, or maybe rolls under the sofa) it's deemed to be Out of Bounds and you must replay the shot from its original position under a penalty of one stroke.

- Play hard but play fair, and whatever the result, shake hands at the end and offer to buy the victor a drink at an improvised nineteenth hole.

- Aside from these rules, it's a question of using the miniature clubs to get the ball in the hole in the fewest number of strokes. Simple, huh?

Tips and tricks

There are a few ways in which you can tip the balance of the match game in your favor. The first is practice. Get to know the quirks of your home course—the powerful draft that blows across the sixth fairway, the crafty knack of

finding the seventeenth green via the corner of the living room fireplace, and so on—and then invite opponents over for a game.

Using a cut-down pencil for a tee will enable you to smash away long drives on the par fives, setting you up to hit the green in two shots. But if you prefer simply to spoil the game of your opponents rather than improving your own, a well-timed sneeze at the top of your opponent's backswing usually helps.

Course Design

In reality, with the *Desktop Golf* kit you have just one green fairway, so you may think that course design is ambitious. However, there are ways of competing in your own version of the four major championships in the comfort of your home. To recreate the visual splendor of Augusta in April, intersperse your holes with flowering potted plants. For the US Open in June— a tournament renowned for its tight fairways—choose a narrow hallway, where space is at a premium. Come July and the British Open, more dedicated players might be tempted to rip up the carpet and play on the floorboards to replicate the fast-running, parched fairways synonymous with that tournament. The last of the season's four majors, the USPGA, is played in August and is often held in southern states where humidity is very high. So, place some wet towels on the radiator and turn the heat up.

FUN GOLF FACTS

▼

- Early shepherds used their curved staffs to hit stones as long ago as 2,000 years—probably the earliest incarnation of golf.

- The first golf balls were made of thin leather and stuffed with feathers. Tightly packed feathers made balls that flew far, but they often split open in wet weather. These "feather-ies" were used until 1848.

- The oldest golf course in the world is The Old Links at Musselburgh, Scotland, where golf has been played since 1672.
- The lowest single-hole level ever posted in a professional event is a staggering twenty-three by Tommy Armour in the 1972 Shawnee Open. Just the previous week, Armour had won the US Open Championship.
- In the 1932 Walker Cup, the legendary Leonard Crawley hit a wayward shot into the eighteenth green

that resulted in hitting the actual Walker Cup trophy, putting a dent into it.

- The world's longest golf course is the International Golf Club in Bolton, Massachussetts, a long par 77, 8,325 yards from the back tees.
- The longest hole in the world is the seventh hole (par 7) of the Sano Course at the Satsuki Golf Club in Japan. It measures 909 yards.

This book as been bound using handcraft methods and Smyth-sewn to ensure durability.

Designed by Jason Kayser

Written by Chris Stone

Edited by Laura Ward and Cindy De La Hoz

The text was set in Chronicle and Verlag.